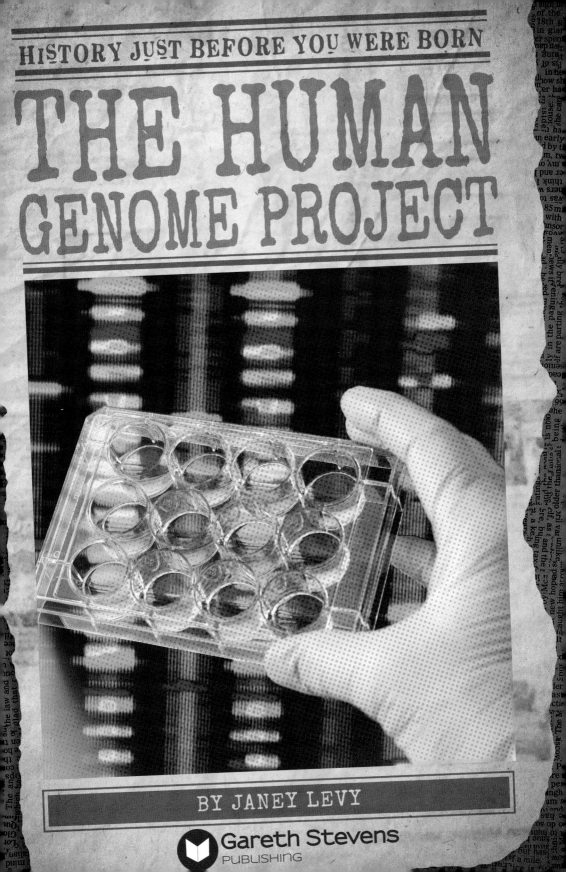

HISTORY JUST BEFORE YOU WERE BORN

THE HUMAN GENOME PROJECT

BY JANEY LEVY

Gareth Stevens
PUBLISHING

Please visit our website, www.garethstevens.com. For a free color catalog of all our high-quality books, call toll free 1-800-542-2595 or fax 1-877-542-2596.

Library of Congress Cataloging-in-Publication Data

Names: Levy, Janey, author.
Title: The Human Genome Project / Janey Levy.
Description: New York : Gareth Stevens Publishing, [2019] | Series: History just before you were born | Includes index.
Identifiers: LCCN 2018017386 | ISBN 9781538230282 (library bound) | ISBN 9781538231371 (paperback) | ISBN 9781538233177 (6 pack)
Subjects: LCSH: Human Genome Project--Juvenile literature. | Human gene mapping--Juvenile literature. | Human genome--Juvenile literature.
Classification: LCC QH445.2 .L49 2019 | DDC 611/.0181663--dc23
LC record available at https://lccn.loc.gov/2018017386

First Edition

Published in 2019 by
Gareth Stevens Publishing
111 East 14th Street, Suite 349
New York, NY 10003

Designer: Sarah Liddell
Editor: Therese Shea

Photo credits: Cover, p. 1 Andrew Brookes/Cultura/Getty Images; newspaper text background used throughout EddieCloud/Shutterstock.com; newspaper shape used throughout AVS-Images/Shutterstock.com; newspaper texture used throughout Here/Shutterstock.com; halftone texture used throughout xpixel/Shutterstock.com; p. 5 (Francis Collins) Ted Thai/Contributor/The LIFE Picture Collection/Getty Images; p. 5 (DNA) Macrovector/Shutterstock.com; p. 7 Science & Society Picture Library/Contributor/SSPL/Getty Images; p. 9 (protein synthesis) BSIP/Contributor/Universal Images Group/Getty Images; p. 9 (karyotype) Earthsound/Wikimedia Commons; p. 11 Sovfoto/Contributor/Universal Images Group/Getty Images; p. 12 vchal/Shutterstock.com; p. 13 Pong Wira/Shutterstock.com; p. 14 SCIENCE SOURCE/Science Source/Getty Images; p. 15 Mercurywoodrose/Wikimedia Commons; p. 17 (DNA sequencer) UW/Wikimedia Commons; p. 17 (Frederick Sanger) Materialscientist/Wikimedia Commons; p. 18 Heiti Paves/Shutterstock.com; p. 19 (mouse) Mirko Sobotta/Shutterstock.com; p. 19 (yeast) sruilk/Shutterstock.com; p. 20 The Biochemist Artist/Shutterstock.com; p. 21 (Francis Collins) ROBYN BECK/Staff/AFP/Getty Images; p. 21 (J. Craig Venter) Calliopejen/Wikimedia Commons; p. 23 FRED TANNEAU/Stringer/AFP/Getty Images; p. 24 Christian Science Monitor/Contributor/Christian Science Monitor/Getty Images; p. 25 Jason Butcher/Cultura/Getty Images; p. 27 CaroleGomez/Vetta/Getty Images; p. 28 Anthony Kwan/Bloomberg via Getty Images.

Printed in the United States of America

CPSIA compliance information: Batch #CW19GS: For further information contact Gareth Stevens, New York, New York at 1-800-542-2595.

CONTENTS

Words in the glossary appear in **bold** type
the first time they are used in the text.

WHAT WAS THE HUMAN GENOME PROJECT?

The Human Genome Project, or HGP, was one of the most groundbreaking scientific and medical developments of the late twentieth century. Simply stated, it was an international research program launched in 1990 to map the human genome. It was a massive, difficult project expected to take 15 years.

The HGP began in the United States, with support from the National Institutes of Health (NIH) and the Department of Energy (DOE). Scientists from around the world soon joined the program. Amazingly, the scientists finished mapping the genome 2 years ahead of schedule!

HGP lead scientist Francis Collins compared the genome to a book with many uses: "It's a history book . . . of the journey of our species through time. It's a shop manual, with an incredibly detailed **blueprint** for building every human cell."

MORE TO THE STORY

The DOE first became involved with human genome research in the 1980s. It was trying to find ways to protect the human genome from the damaging effects of **radiation.**

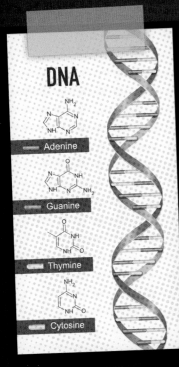

DNA

Adenine

Guanine

Thymine

Cytosine

FRANCIS COLLINS, A MEDICAL DOCTOR WITH A PHD IN PHYSICAL CHEMISTRY, BEGAN DIRECTING THE HUMAN GENOME PROJECT IN 1993. BEFORE JOINING THE PROJECT, COLLINS DID RESEARCH ON GENES RESPONSIBLE FOR SEVERAL DISEASES.

WHAT'S A GENOME?

A genome is an organism's complete set of DNA. DNA contains the instructions necessary for the development of a living thing. It also directs the activities within the organism's body. Each DNA molecule is composed of two twisted, paired strands made up of chemical units known as nucleotide bases. There are four bases: adenine (A), thymine (T), guanine (G), and cytosine (C). The bases always pair in a certain way: A on one strand pairs with T on the opposite strand, and C pairs with G.

WHY DO THE HUMAN GENOME PROJECT?

A question you might be asking now—and one that others asked at the time—is: Why carry out the Human Genome Project in the first place? Research into human genes was already underway. The HGP was expected to take the efforts of many researchers around the world for 15 years. It would require billions of dollars that could go to traditional **biomedical** research, such as the study of human diseases. Would it be worth it?

Most researchers felt it would be. Although many genes had been researched, the majority of the human genome was a mystery. Physicians and scientists recognized the importance of mapping the entire genome and having that knowledge available. It would provide an understanding of the genetic factors in human disease. This was the goal of the HGP.

MORE TO THE STORY

There isn't just one human genome, of course. Every person's genome is a bit different, but all human genomes are very similar. Mapping one (or a few) is helpful for everyone.

MANY HUMAN DISEASES AND CONDITIONS HAVE A GENETIC FACTOR.

GENES AND HEALTH

Have you ever wondered why some people seem to get sick all the time and others hardly ever get sick? Scientists have found that nearly every human disease has some basis in our genes. That's not to say that lifestyle, diet, and **environment** don't have an effect on human health. But their effect is determined by how they interact with a person's genetics. Mapping the human genome helps researchers learn about all aspects of human health and disease.

A SPECIAL LANGUAGE

There's a whole language—a set of special terms—that goes with the Human Genome Project. The study of groups of genes is called genomics. We've already talked about DNA. The word "gene" generally refers to a package of DNA that carries instructions for making a protein or set of proteins. And proteins make up much of the human body! Genes are located on 23 pairs of threadlike structures called chromosomes that are packed into the **nucleus** of each human cell.

In order to map the human genome, researchers had to sequence the DNA. Sequencing means figuring out the exact order of the bases—adenine, thymine, guanine, and cytosine—in a strand of DNA. Sequencing allows researchers to look for mutations, or changes, that may play a part in disease.

MORE TO THE STORY

A mutated gene may produce an abnormal protein, which can lead to disease. The mutation may be as small as exchanging, removing, or adding a pair of bases or as large as excluding thousands of bases.

THIS DRAWING ILLUSTRATES
MESSENGER RNA BEING
TRANSPORTED FROM THE NUCLEUS
TO THE CYTOPLASM WHERE IT'S
"READ" BY A RIBOSOME AND USED
TO MAKE PROTEINS.

THIS IMAGE SHOWS THE
PAIRS OF CHROMOSOMES
BELONGING TO A MAN.

MORE TERMS

How does a gene direct the production of proteins? An enzyme, which is itself a type of protein, copies the gene's information into a molecule called messenger ribonucleic acid, or mRNA. The mRNA leaves the nucleus and enters the surrounding jellylike substance called the cytoplasm. There, it's read by a molecular structure called a ribosome. The information is then used to join the tiny molecules called amino acids in the right order to form a certain protein.

A BRIEF HISTORY OF GENETICS

The HGP wouldn't have been possible without the work of many earlier scientists. The history of genetics began in the mid-1800s with the research of the man known today as the father of genetics—Gregor Mendel.

Mendel didn't know about DNA or chromosomes, but his experiments with garden peas revealed the basic laws of genetics. Mendel's experiments traced the transmission of seven traits, or features, by crossing peas that differed in one trait, such as color. He found that one form of the trait would be dominant and the other would be recessive.

Mendel made no real effort to share his work with the world, and few scientists of the time recognized its importance. His research was rediscovered and appreciated beginning around 1900.

MORE TO THE STORY

The patterns of the transmission of traits that Mendel discovered are now called "Mendelian inheritance" in his honor.

GREGOR MENDEL WAS, PERHAPS SURPRISINGLY, A MONK. HE GREW UP ON A SMALL FARM IN AN AREA THAT'S NOW PART OF THE CZECH REPUBLIC. THE LOCAL PRIEST RECOGNIZED HIS INTELLIGENCE AND SUGGESTED THAT HE GO AWAY TO SCHOOL AT THE AGE OF 11.

DOMINANT AND RECESSIVE GENES

This example shows how Mendel discovered dominant and recessive traits: When he crossed purple-flowered peas with white-flowered peas, all the plants in the next generation had purple flowers. But when he bred the peas from that second generation with each other, some plants in the third generation had white flowers. So Mendel knew those plants still carried the instructions for making white flowers, but those instructions were hidden. He called the purple trait "dominant" and the white trait "recessive."

Another big achievement in genetics came in 1913. That year, a young student at Columbia University in New York City published the world's first genetic map.

The student, Alfred Sturtevant, was working in the research laboratory of geneticist Thomas Hunt Morgan. Morgan used the fruit fly *Drosophila melanogaster* to research **heredity**. The lab, filled with millions of fruit flies, was known as the Fly Room.

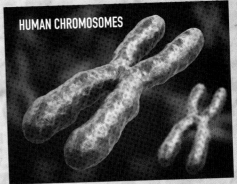

HUMAN CHROMOSOMES

Sturtevant's map showed all the genes of the fruit fly in their correct positions. He showed that genes are set out in a linear arrangement along chromosomes. He also revealed that the gene for any specific trait has a fixed location, or locus, on its chromosome. His remarkable work opened the door for genetic maps of other species.

MORE TO THE STORY

When Sturtevant got the idea for his map, he was so excited he stayed up all night working on it. He made his genetic map instead of doing his homework!

WHY *DROSOPHILA MELANOGASTER?*

Why did Morgan use fruit flies to study heredity? These creatures have several qualities that make them the perfect organisms for such studies. They only live 10 days, so researchers quickly have several generations to study. They're very fertile, so researchers can produce millions of them. They only have four pairs of chromosomes to understand. And they're tiny, so they don't take up much space.

IF YOU'VE EVER HAD FRESH FRUIT SITTING OUT IN YOUR KITCHEN AT HOME, YOU'RE LIKELY FAMILIAR WITH TINY FRUIT FLIES.

Another big development happened in 1953, when the molecular structure of DNA was described. Two teams in England were racing to be the first to discover DNA's structure: James Watson and Francis Crick at Cambridge University and Maurice Wilkins and Rosalind Franklin at King's College London.

ROSALIND FRANKLIN

Both teams published articles in the same issue of the journal *Nature*. They proposed that DNA's structure was a double helix. That means it looks like a ladder that's been twisted into a curling shape. This structure matched the existing experimental data so perfectly that it was soon accepted as correct. In 1962, Watson, Crick, and Wilkins shared the Nobel Prize in Physiology or Medicine for their discovery. Franklin, who died in 1958, wasn't included.

MORE TO THE STORY

Watson, Crick, Wilkins, and Franklin laid the foundation for the field of molecular biology, the science that investigates the structure of large molecules (such as DNA and proteins) of living matter and their part in biological processes.

UNSUNG HERO

Scientist Rosalind Franklin used **X-rays** to create images of DNA. Her coworker, Maurice Wilkins, showed one image, known as Photograph 51, to scientist James Watson without her permission. Watson said, "My jaw fell open and my pulse began to race." It inspired his work with Francis Crick. When Watson and Crick published their findings, they acknowledged Franklin's work. However, she died of cancer at the age of 37 in 1958, before she could receive the recognition the other scientists did.

PHOTOGRAPH 51

MILESTONES IN DNA RESEARCH

RESEARCHERS	DATE FINDINGS PUBLISHED	EVENT
FRIEDRICH MIESCHER	1869	DISCOVERED DNA
PHOEBUS LEVENE	1919	IDENTIFIED PARTS OF DNA MOLECULE
OSWALD AVERY AND ROCKEFELLER UNIVERSITY RESEARCHERS	1944	SHOWED GENES ARE COMPOSED OF DNA
ERWIN CHARGAFF	1950	FOUND THAT USUALLY IN DNA AMOUNTS OF A AND T ARE EQUAL AND AMOUNTS OF G AND C ARE EQUAL
JAMES WATSON AND FRANCIS CRICK; MAURICE WILKINS AND ROSALIND FRANKLIN	1953	DISCOVERED THE DOUBLE-HELIX STRUCTURE OF DNA

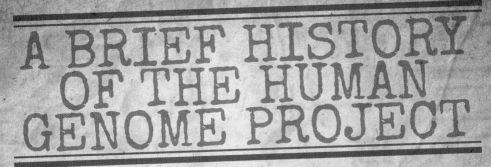

A BRIEF HISTORY OF THE HUMAN GENOME PROJECT

In the mid-1970s, Frederick Sanger developed methods for sequencing DNA. When **automated** DNA sequencing machines were introduced in the 1980s, some biologists proposed investigating the entire human genome. This might be said to mark the birth of the Human Genome Project.

It was also in the 1980s that the DOE was looking for data on how to protect the human genome from mutations caused by radiation. In 1987, the DOE established a genome project. The following year, Congress gave money to both the DOE and the NIH to begin work on a genome project. James Watson was chosen to head the project at the NIH. By 1990, the planning stage was complete.

MORE TO THE STORY

In 1986, the company Applied Biosystems began to produce DNA sequencing machines. This **technology** used dyes to mark each nucleotide, so the results could be read using colors. The machines read 12,000 DNA "letters" per day.

FREDERICK SANGER

DNA SEQUENCING MACHINES

FOR HIS WORK SEQUENCING DNA, SANGER RECEIVED THE NOBEL PRIZE IN CHEMISTRY IN 1980.

CHANGING NAMES, CHANGING LEADERS

When Watson was appointed to head the NIH project, an office was also set up. It was first called the Office of Human Genome Research, but it soon became the National Center for Human Genome Research. Then, in 1997, it became the National Human Genome Research Institute. Along the way, there were also changes in the project's leader. Watson resigned in 1992 and was replaced by an acting director. Francis Collins became director in 1993 and remained until the project was completed.

You might be surprised to learn the HGP didn't dive right into sequencing and mapping the human genome. The researchers had a lot of other work they had to do first. Much of their early efforts were devoted to developing improved technologies for sequencing the genome more quickly.

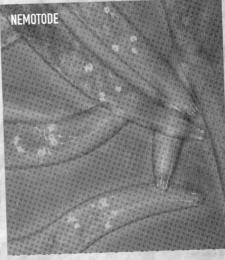

NEMOTODE

In 1993, when Francis Collins became director, a special division was set up to develop genome technology and study certain diseases. As Collins later wrote, "Building detailed genetic and physical maps, developing better, cheaper and faster technologies for handling DNA, and mapping and sequencing the more modest-sized genomes of **model organisms** were all critical stepping stones on the path to initiating the large-scale sequencing of the human genome."

MORE TO THE STORY

Not even the volunteers who gave their blood for the HGP know if their samples were used!

WHOSE DNA WAS USED IN THE HGP?

A decision was made to use **anonymous**, representative samples of DNA for the project. So the mapped genome isn't DNA from one person, but from several people. The DNA came from blood samples provided by volunteers at several different locations. Blood was taken from almost 100 volunteers, but only a small number of the samples were actually used for the project. The names of the volunteers were removed before the samples were chosen for sequencing.

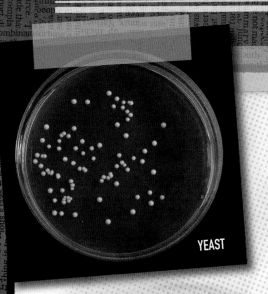

YEAST

MICE, YEAST, AND NEMOTODES ARE SOME OF THE MODEL ORGANISMS USED IN GENETIC RESEARCH.

In February 2001, about 90 percent of the genome's sequence was published in the journal *Nature*. But this form of the genome contained over 150,000 gaps. In April 2003, the final finished genome sequence was announced. However, there were still nearly 400 gaps. Why was this?

The human genome has 3 billion base pairs. To sequence the genome, DNA was cut into small sections. Sections overlapped on purpose so computers could order the sections by matching up the overlaps. However, certain sections with repeating segments were difficult to put in order, which created gaps in the entire sequence. Today, some scientists want to fill in the gaps, but new technologies need to be invented to handle the task.

COMPUTER IMAGE OF PART OF THE HUMAN GENOME

MORE TO THE STORY

HGP scientists figured out which bases made up genes. Estimates for the number of human genes once ranged from 50,000 to 140,000. The HGP showed the actual number was around 20,000!

COMPETITOR AND ALLY

In 1998, geneticist J. Craig Venter founded a company later called Celera Genomics to sequence the human genome. He thought the HGP was taking too long and costing too much. He also thought the information should be available only to paying customers. The HGP and Celera Genomics raced to finish first. In June 2000, it was announced both groups had sequenced a majority of the genome—they had both won. After that, they worked together.

J. CRAIG VENTER

ON APRIL 14, 2003, FRANCIS COLLINS ANNOUNCED THAT RESEARCHERS HAD SUCCESSFULLY COMPLETED A MAP OF THE HUMAN GENOME—2 YEARS EARLIER THAN EXPECTED.

THE HUMAN GENOME PROJECT'S IMPACT

The HGP has already had an enormous effect on medical research and treatment of diseases. It's led to the discovery of over 1,800 disease genes. Researchers can find a gene suspected of causing an inherited disease in days rather than the years it once took. Over 2,000 genetic tests for human conditions now exist. They allow people to learn their genetic risk for these conditions and help doctors **diagnose** diseases. The HGP is aiding in studies of rare diseases, too.

Great progress has also been made in a new field called pharmacogenomics. This field looks at how a person's genetic makeup affects their response to a drug, and it allows physicians to decide on the best drug and dose to give a patient.

THIS RESEARCHER AT A LAB IN FRANCE IS TESTING A DRUG BEING DEVELOPED TO FIGHT THE GENETIC DISORDER KNOWN AS CYSTIC FIBROSIS.

THE INTERNATIONAL HAPMAP PROJECT

The International HapMap Project was one outcome of the HGP. This project included researchers from the United States and five other countries in an effort to record common genetic variations, called haplotypes, in the human genome. The researchers studied populations from around the world and helped identify genetic factors that play a part in several conditions, such as blindness. The project also helped researchers understand how genetic differences affect individuals' response to drugs.

It might surprise you to learn the HGP has also had a huge effect on the law. Information from the human genome sequence, examined through a system called CODIS (Combined DNA Index System), has dramatically changed the field known as forensic medicine. This is the science that deals with the application of medical facts to legal matters, including crimes. DNA has made it possible to positively identify criminals from very tiny samples of biological matter, such as spit, hairs, or a spot of dried blood.

In criminal cases, DNA can prove innocence as well as guilt. DNA evidence has been used to prove the innocence of men and women wrongfully convicted for crimes they didn't commit, sometimes many years after they were convicted.

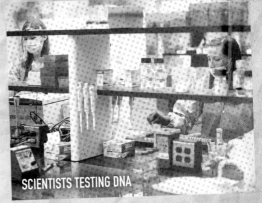
SCIENTISTS TESTING DNA

MORE TO THE STORY

DNA studies have allowed scientists to confirm that the modern human species, *Homo sapiens*, arose in Africa about 200,000 years ago.

THE INNOCENCE PROJECT

In 1992, Peter Neufeld and Barry Scheck founded the Innocence Project at Cardozo School of Law at Yeshiva University in New York City. The project's purpose is to use DNA testing of previously collected evidence to prove the innocence of people who have been wrongly convicted. So far, DNA has allowed the project to prove over 350 people innocent and has also helped identify more than 100 people who actually committed crimes.

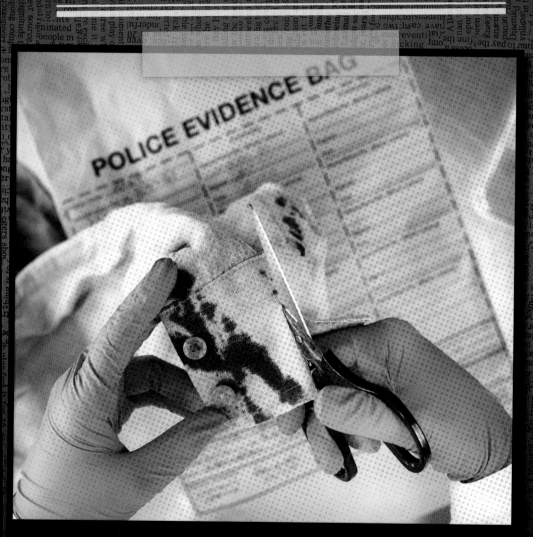

THE BLOOD ON THIS SHIRT MAY YIELD VALUABLE EVIDENCE IN A POLICE INVESTIGATION.

A BRAVE NEW WORLD

Building on the HGP, the National Human Genome Research Institute and the National Cancer Institute (NCI) began the Cancer Genome Atlas (TCGA) in 2005. By the time TCGA concluded in 2017, it had produced maps of the key genomic changes in 33 types of cancer. Even though TCGA has ended, the kind of research TCGA carried out is being continued by the NCI Center for Cancer Genomics (CCG). The CCG studies cancer genomics in several areas and shares its findings with other researchers.

Knowing the genomic changes that cause a disease such as cancer allows researchers and physicians to develop more effective treatments for the disease. That can mean developing new drugs rather than relying on traditional treatments such as radiation and powerful chemicals.

MORE TO THE STORY

Knowledge of cancer genomics has already allowed researchers to develop a drug to treat a certain type of lung cancer.

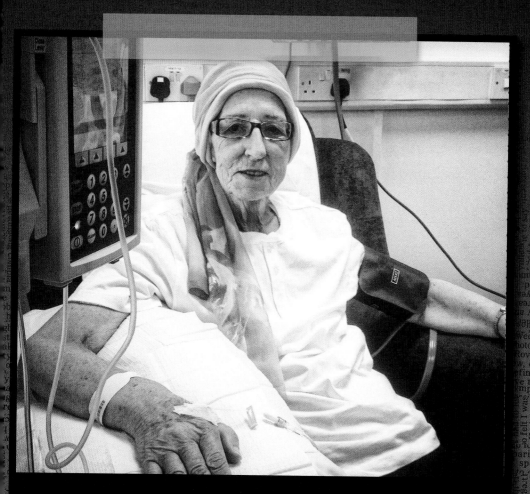

TRADITIONAL CANCER TREATMENTS CAN CAUSE A PERSON'S HAIR TO FALL OUT AND CAN BE VERY HARD ON THE HUMAN BODY. THE HOPE IS THAT NEW, MORE EFFECTIVE TREATMENTS WILL HAVE FEWER SUCH EFFECTS AND TARGET CANCER CELLS MORE DIRECTLY.

A LONG ROAD

New drugs don't come on the market too quickly. Once drug companies have the genomic knowledge, they must do research to develop the drugs. Then they must test the drugs in laboratory animals to see if they work and are safe. Finally, they must do what are called clinical trials. They test the drugs on human volunteers to make sure they work on humans and are safe. This whole process can take 10 to 15 years.

Our ability to sequence the human genome has changed dramatically since the days of the HGP. A British company called Oxford Nanopore developed a device about the size of a cell phone that can sequence the genome. Just imagine—instead of needing hundreds of millions of dollars, researchers around the world, and 13 years, all that's needed is a device you can hold in your hand! Companies today are racing to sequence DNA even more quickly and cheaply.

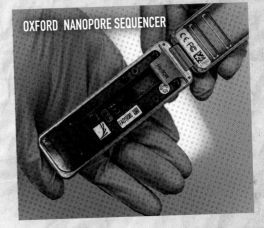

OXFORD NANOPORE SEQUENCER

No one can say for sure what the future holds. But the knowledge gained from the Human Genome Project has already dramatically changed science, medicine, and the legal field. More changes are certain to come. Perhaps you'll play a part in creating those changes!

MORE TO THE STORY

The Oxford Nanopore device was used to track the spread of a terrible disease called Ebola in western Africa.

OTHER CONSIDERATIONS

Sequencing an individual's genome can let them learn about their genetic risks, helping them plan and prepare for treatment. But can it also have harmful consequences? What if employers and insurance companies use the information to treat the person unfairly? In order to figure out ways to address these and other concerns, the Ethical, Legal, and Social Implications (ELSI) Research Program was established at the beginning of the HGP. It still exists as part of the National Human Genome Research Institute.

A TIMELINE OF THE HUMAN GENOME PROJECT

1866: GREGOR MENDEL PUBLISHES THE RESULTS OF HIS EXPERIMENTS.

1869: FRIEDRICH MIESCHER REPORTS DISCOVERING DNA.

1913: ALFRED STURTEVANT PUBLISHES THE WORLD'S FIRST GENETIC MAP.

1919: PHOEBUS LEVENE PUBLISHES RESEARCH ABOUT THE PARTS OF DNA.

1944: OSWALD AVERY DIRECTS RESEARCH THAT SHOWS GENES ARE COMPOSED OF DNA.

1950: ERWIN CHARGAFF EXPLAINS THE AMOUNTS OF A AND T ARE EQUAL AND AMOUNTS OF G AND C ARE EQUAL IN DNA.

1953: JAMES WATSON AND FRANCIS CRICK, ALONG WITH MAURICE WILKINS AND ROSALIND FRANKLIN, ANNOUNCE THE DISCOVERY OF THE DOUBLE-HELIX STRUCTURE OF DNA.

MID-1970s: FREDERICK SANGER DEVELOPS METHODS FOR SEQUENCING DNA.

1980s: DNA SEQUENCING BECOMES AUTOMATED.

1987: THE DOE ESTABLISHES AN EARLY GENOME PROJECT.

1988: CONGRESS GIVES MONEY TO THE DOE AND NIH FOR A GENOME PROJECT.

1990: THE PLANNING STAGE FOR THE HGP IS COMPLETE.

1998: J. CRAIG VENTER FOUNDS CELERA GENOMICS TO SEQUENCE THE HUMAN GENOME.

2000: THE MAJORITY OF THE HUMAN GENOME IS SEQUENCED BY BOTH HGP AND CELERA GENOMICS.

2002: THE INTERNATIONAL HAPMAP PROJECT BEGINS.

2003: THE FINAL FINISHED GENOME SEQUENCE IS ANNOUNCED.

2005: THE CANCER GENOME ATLAS BEGINS.

2015: OXFORD NANOPORE'S HANDHELD DEVICE FOR SEQUENCING THE HUMAN GENOME IS SUCCESSFULLY TESTED.

GLOSSARY

anonymous: not named or identified

automated: run or operated by machines or computers rather than people

biomedical: having to do with biological, medical, and physical science

blueprint: a detailed plan of how to do something

complex: having to do with something with many parts that work together

diagnose: to recognize a disease or illness by examining someone

environment: the conditions that surround a living thing and affect the way it lives

heredity: the natural process by which physical and mental qualities are passed from a parent to a child

model organism: a species that has been widely studied, usually because it is easy to maintain and breed in a laboratory setting

nucleus: the central part of most cells that contains genetic material and is enclosed in a membrane

radiation: a type of dangerous and powerful energy that is produced by certain substances and nuclear reactions

technology: tools, machines, or ways to do things that use the latest discoveries to fix problems or meet needs

X-ray: a powerful type of energy that is similar to light but is invisible to the human eye

FOR MORE INFORMATION

BOOKS

Arbuthnott, Gill. *What Makes You You?* New York, NY: Crabtree Publishing Company, 2016.

Ballen, Karen Gunnison. *Decoding Our DNA: Craig Venter vs the Human Genome Project*. Minneapolis, MN: Twenty-First Century Books, 2013.

Mitchell, Megan. *The Human Genome*. New York, NY: Cavendish Square, 2017.

WEBSITES

A Brief History from Mendel to the Human Genome Project
unlockinglifescode.org/timeline
This site offers an interactive timeline—with photos—that traces the history of genetics from Gregor Mendel to the Human Genome Project.

Who Was Involved in the Human Genome Project?
www.yourgenome.org/stories/who-was-involved-in-the-human-genome-project
Learn more about the groups of scientists around the world who took part in the Human Genome Project on this site.

INDEX